After Goodbye

After Goodbye

HOW TO BEGIN AGAIN
AFTER THE DEATH OF SOMEONE YOU LOVE

TED MENTEN

RUNNING PRESS
PHILADELPHIA · LONDON

18 17 16 15 14 13 12
Digit on the right indicates the number of this printing.

Library of Congress Cataloging-in-Publication Number 93–85506

ISBN 1–56138–295–7

Cover design by Toby Schmidt
Interior design by Christian Benton
Cover illustration by Jennifer Heyd Wharton
Typography: ITC Berkeley with Poppl-Residenz Light
by Deborah Lugar

This book may be ordered by mail from the publisher.
Please add $2.50 for postage and handling.
But try your bookstore first!
Running Press Book Publishers
125 South Twenty-second Street
Philadelphia, Pennsylvania 19103–4399

This book is dedicated

to the memory of

my grandmother,

Laura Menten,

who taught me that

life is filled with wonder

and that death is not

something to be frightened

of, but rather the one who

taps you on the shoulder

and asks for the last waltz,

twirling you away in the

final dance of life.

CONTENTS

PREFACE

My friend Greg was a genius in the kitchen. As pots bubbled and the oven emitted aromas that made my palate yearn, he often mused about the wonders of foods and their preparation.

"A good sauce keeps getting better with time. Like a good wine." He'd bend over a steaming pot and wave the fragrances toward his expert nostrils, and then frown—pondering (I supposed) the age-old quandary of whether it needed more salt.

"Pasta sauces are always better a day or so later," he once said. "Of course you may want to add a little of this or that to perk it up, or personalize it to the pasta you're serving."

I wondered how you would personalize a pasta sauce. I decided that if you add a little of this or that, suddenly the pasta becomes special with a sauce all its own.

With that in mind, I'd like to reheat a little sauce of my own. Since you may be sitting down with me for the first time as you read this book, I thought I'd share with you what I've learned. You don't have to believe what I believe, or question what I question, or even come to any of the same conclusions. We'll just walk together and talk things over.

I believe that there is a supreme being, a creator, because when I look around at the wonder and beauty of life, I can find no other reasonable explanation.

I like the idea of prayer. I think it is more sane to talk to someone else than it is to talk to yourself. (At first I had a problem with unanswered prayers until Susan, age seven, explained it to me: "That's simple: God's answer was, 'No.')

I like ghosts and reincarnation, too. A mystic once described my grandmother as an aura that followed me and protected me. That seems right enough; it's what she did before she died. I support recycling, so I suppose it is only natural to accept reincarnation.

Heaven is a good idea, too. I like reunions; I like all the hugging and kissing and tears of joy when old friends get back together.

I believe that love gives the best return on investment.

I believe that truth is like a straight line—the shortest distance between two points.

I believe in second chances, and third chances, and fourth chances.

I believe that listening is essential to loving.

I believe that a loving silence is more golden than a thoughtless platitude.

I believe in grief and sorrow and wailing, and tears flowing like Niagara Falls. Tears mean something. They mean we're alive and feeling.

I believe that death is a friend, a fabulous dancer who will twirl me away in my last waltz.

I believe that the only real death is being forgotten.

I believe in taking time to say goodbye, and not putting it off until another day.

I believe that taking the first step is the most important thing we can do. And more than anything,

I believe in love.

—Ted Menten

ACKNOWLEDGMENTS

Writing a book is like chicken soup, and the author is only one of the ingredients. Here is the complete recipe.

First, the people who form the base—the stock—who shared their stories and their lives with me during long walks and sessions in Harmony.

Next, add all the people at Running Press who ordered the soup in the first place, and added direction and wisdom as it simmered its way to completion. Especially my editor, David Borgenicht, who made sure everything was blended and seasoned to just the right flavor.

And then there are all the tasters, who read the manuscript in bits and pieces and added their own spicy comments along the way: Cissy, Chuck, Diane, Dave, Marc, Jane, David, and Thor.

Thanks.

INTRODUCTION

I had just won the fifty million-dollar lottery when the jangling sound of the phone shattered my dream and brought me back to harsh reality. I reached for the phone and glanced at the glowing numerals on my digital clock: 3 A.M.

"Is this Mister Silly?" asked an unfamiliar voice.

"Yes, it is," I replied, trying not to sound too grumpy.

"I have a patient here who demands to see you. He says that he is dying."

"Is he?" I asked.

"I don't know that," she snapped. "I'm just the night nurse."

"I'll be there in twenty minutes."

"Are you a doctor?" she asked, in a confused voice.

"No," I replied, "but you can clear it with the head nurse."

I have made this kind of late night run a hundred times or more. Sometimes, the patient *has* actually been dying, but usually it's a false alarm. While I was dreaming about winning the lottery, some frightened child had a visitation from the boogeyman—and thought it was death.

I approached the nurses' station and came face to face with a young, very starched, nurse with tightly pursed lips and a frown that threatened to make a permanent groove on her face. Her I.D. tag read: Nurse Martin.

"Hi, I'm Mister Silly," I announced with a smile.

"Follow me," she ordered, and set off down the hall. "Try not to upset him, please," she snapped. "I've had just about enough of this nonsense for one night." She opened the door for me, turned away, and returned to her station.

"Mister Silly?" a small voice called out. "Is that you?"

"Yes, it is. What's this about dying, young man?"

"I saw death, Mister Silly. He was right at the foot of my bed and he wanted to take me away with him. I said no, but he said he'd be back to get me, and I'm scared."

"Well, you've had quite an adventure haven't you? A visit from death and a promise that he'll be back seems pretty scary to me. Did he tell you when he'd be back?"

"No, but I think he meant soon—maybe tomorrow."

"Well," I sat on the edge of the bed next to my eight-year-old little buddy, "How about I give you a big hug and hold you for a while so things won't seem so scary, and you can tell me what else death had to say." Timmy crawled into my arms and held on to me very tightly.

"He was all dark and hidden and had a whispery

voice, and he said it was time for me to die and he had come to get me and I was real scared and I said 'No, no, no, I don't want to go'—and I called the nurse and asked her to get you. Is that OK?"

"Sure. Then what happened?"

"He went away when the nurse came, but I think he was only hiding from her. I need you to chase him away, Mister Silly—you can do that can't you?"

"No, Timmy, I can't. You see when death really does come no one can chase him away. But I don't think that was death that came to see you. I think that was just Mister Nightmare who likes to scare little guys like you, and even big guys like me. He knows what frightens us, so he climbs into our dreams and messes everything up. But that isn't what death is like—you know that don't you? We've talked about death and how he is the conductor that takes us on our last journey. He's not such a bad guy. He just has a difficult job. Remember?"

"But he said he was death!"

"It was just a trick to scare you, Timmy. Now go back to sleep and dream nice things and don't be afraid. OK?"

"OK?"

"And I'll sit right here and make sure that Mister Nightmare doesn't come back again."

"Thanks, Mister Silly."

About five minutes later my little buddy was back in dreamland. I straightened his covers, brushed back his hair, and kissed him goodnight.

I closed the door quietly and headed back down the hall to the nurses' station.

"He's asleep again. I think he'll be OK, now."

"Just who are you, anyway?" Nurse Martin snapped. "Everyone around here just says to give you whatever you want. I don't understand."

"I'm Mister Silly, the court jester—the fool—the clown. In the days of King Arthur, only Merlin the Wizard and the court jester could tell the king the truth without fear of retaliation or punishment. That's what I do with these kids who are dying. I tell them the truth—and then I fall down and make them laugh. I steal their fear and give them a giggle. Not too complicated really unless you've forgotten how to laugh. Have you forgotten, Nurse Martin?"

"Terminal children are hardly a laughing matter."

"On the contrary—that is exactly what they are. They are not to be pitied or pampered or indulged or even treated as if they are different. They are still children, and they need to be laughed *with*. They are very much about laughter."

• • •

Several months later, death came for Timmy and took him away. I was with him when death came, and he wasn't the dark creature that had come to call that other time. Timmy told me that death was white and bright and pretty. And then he was gone. I miss him.

When I began working with terminal children, I realized very quickly how little laughter was being prescribed by their physicians. I bumped up their daily dosage, and earned the name of Mister Silly.

Death is not a laughing matter, but I learned long ago that laughter can be a balm that soothes. When someone we love dies, we must find our way out of our grief and back into life.

Perhaps a gentle clown is a good companion on that journey. I hope so.

PROLOGUE

In *Gentle Closings* I described the process of saying goodbye to a loved one who is dying by imagining couples parting in a railroad station.

> If you have ever stood in a busy railroad station and watched people leave one another, you may have noticed that no two couples say goodbye in exactly the same way —but each does it perfectly. Some hug and laugh. Some cling silently to one another with tears streaming down their cheeks. Some simply hold hands and gaze into one another's eyes, remembering the good times before this moment. And when it's time to leave, they take one long, last look, and then they let go.

Now, one partner has gone, and left the other behind. The one who remains is left standing alone on the station platform, waving goodbye to an ever-diminishing puff of smoke as the train vanishes into the horizon. A thousand books and films have depicted this scene. Often, the scene is then imprinted with the legend "The End."

But is it?

We do not know much about the destination called death, or about the afterlife. But we do know a great deal about its counterparts—life and afterdeath.

This book is about Life and Afterdeath.

If we return to the train station platform we see what happens to the people who have been left behind. Each person reacts differently. One stands transfixed, tears streaming down, heart pounding, stomach in knots, fists clenched in agony. Another wanders aimlessly, numb and drained, blind with pain. Still another crumples to the floor. Everywhere there is pain and sorrow—or so it might seem.

But one woman squares her shoulders, picks up her baggage, and heads for another departure gate. Her destination is called *Life*.

This book is about that journey—the journey out of grieving, back into Life.

PART ONE:
Questions

SOLITAIRE

Louise Nevelson, the powerfully creative, grande dame of American sculptors, once described her life status not as "single," or "unmarried," but simply, as a "solitaire." I was delighted by the image because it had such a positive flavor.

Solitaire is a game of cards for one, but it is also a single gem, often a diamond, set by itself.

In my single days I described myself as "going solo," a term I learned from my parents, who were both pilots. In flight terms, flying solo is a singular achievement—a high point.

In our society, there are a number of forms of partnership. Webster's defines a "widow" as a woman who has outlived her husband, but the current politically correct fashion of language encourages us to render all terms gender-free. With this in mind, I began using the term widow to include both men and women, married or unmarried, straight or gay. There was some resistance at first among those who heard the word used in a new way, but it was enlightening for everyone to see how similar their reactions to the death of a partner were, whatever their gender or sexual orientation. As with any dissolved twosome, there was a sense of one half remaining and the other half being lost.

We often hear a woman say, "I lost my husband," when in fact she had nothing to do with his death. But if she said, "My husband left me," people would conclude that her husband had abandoned her.

Socially conventional language often masks the truth of a situation. We are encouraged to express one thing by saying another. The problem is that we all look for comfortable ways to speak about uncomfortable things. We have real difficulty saying, "I am sorry your partner died."

Why?

Almost everyone has difficulty with the words "death" and "dying." We use other words like "terminal," which has a meaning just as terrifying, but is somehow easier to say and hear. Kids and adults alike treat the "d" word with as much disdain as the "f" word. I call these Ostrich Maneuvers, because they keep our awareness in the sand. If we don't use the "d" word it won't happen—or so we hope.

When women who have lost their partners discuss their lack of identity they say, "Who am I now? I used to be Mrs. Robert Johnson or Betty Johnson. Who am I now—the Widow Johnson? Who is that?" And when they come to that question, I tell them about Louise Nevelson and the life of a solitaire.

A person who has been in a partnership is considerably different from a person who has been going solo. Partners depend on each other to carry at least half of life's burdens. Income, labor, children, and pleasure are just a few of the experiences that are no longer shared when a partnership ends. But while I encourage widows to become a solitaire in their own right, I do not encourage them to play the game of life like a game of solitaire.

When we suddenly find ourselves going solo, we have to learn to rethink our lives, and consider the game from both sides of the board—kind of a chess game for one.

For in the new game of solo living, all the moves are yours.

THE WHY OF DEATH

When we hear the phrase, "There are no easy answers," it usually means that we are about to hear to an evasive, roundabout explanation to a perfectly simple question such as, "What is the meaning of life?" Or,

"What is the meaning of death?"

Often, the answer to a question is contained within the question itself. For instance, the question, "What can you do?" is easily answered by simply rearranging the same words—"Do what you can." Sometimes there *are* easy answers, and they are very often exactly right.

Even that timeless and complex question about the meaning of life has an answer within itself. Here we cannot simply rearrange the words, but we can answer the question by rearranging the idea within it.

Question: What is the meaning of life?

Answer: That life have meaning.

Now we need to define the word *meaning*. That's also easy—because there is no one answer. Each person has a personal answer to what gives life meaning.

So we have to personalize the question to, "What is the meaning of *my* life?" and the answer, "That my life have meaning."

By making an abstract, philosophical question both simple and personal we get an uncomplicated, personal answer.

The next obvious step might be to apply that same process to the second question, "What is the meaning of death?" OK, let's try it.

Question: What is the meaning of *my* death?

Answer: That my death have meaning.

Hmmm. That isn't quite the answer most of us are looking for. That's the stuff of heroes and legends, and most of us aren't thinking in heroic terms.

When I was a little boy I asked my father, an electronics whiz, why the lights went on when I flipped the switch. He was able to tell me *how*, but no matter how hard he tried, he couldn't tell me exactly *why*. Children make adults crazy with that question: Why? Why? Why?

In fact, we all drive each other crazy with that question. As far as I can tell, God is asked that question about a trillion times every millisecond. In the end, there is no answer—it is almost always a matter of faith, of believing in the process. I now know how the lights go on when I flip the switch, and I have faith in the process.

But I never—ever—asked why they went out when I flipped the switch in the opposite direction. The answer to the first question automatically provided the answer to the second.

So perhaps if we understand and accept the answer to the question, "What is the meaning of my life?" we won't need to ask, "What is the meaning of my death?"

Both children and adults ask, "Why did [a loved one]

die?" There are no answers to this question either. We die for exactly the same reason we live—because we can. That is the process. That is the why of it. A woman gives birth because she can. We live because our mechanism enables us to. And we die because we can. That's the system. Just like the light switch. It does what it does and we do what we do.

When we ask why someone we love has died we are asking a series of questions that are not so easily answered. When a child asks about death, other questions are really being asked. For example, "Why did Mommy die (now)?" or "Why did Mommy die (and leave me)?"

Come to think of it, isn't that the real question we ask when a loved one dies? "Why now?" "Why me?" Whatever questions we ask, we are expressing loss—our loss. Grief is essentially about loss. Listen to the words: "What a terrible loss." "There was so much he wanted to do." "We'll all miss her."

When we say goodbye to a loved one, we experience a loving closing. And when they are gone, we experience loss—and we call that loss *grief*.

In that moment and the moments that follow, all the answers in the world don't matter. We don't really care *why*—because it really wouldn't help.

Shadows and Rainbows

Memories can be rainbows one day and stalking shadow nightmares the next.

When we are in a loving relationship we make memories automatically—by being alive together. Minute by minute, our lives create millions of impressions that are stored in our memory. When lovers first meet, they may stand under an umbrella and kiss. Later, after their courtship has progressed, they once again cuddle in the rain and remember that first time. That memory is a rainbow, from start to finish. But once a partner has died, all that may be left is the memory of that first kiss in the rain.

It may hurt to remember. It may heal to remember. It's hard to know what the effect will be—the nature of healing is as elusive as the nature of pain. Sometimes pain is healing, and sometimes healing is painful.

But I encourage the creation of memories because I believe in the human heart and the human spirit. I believe that we have the innate ability to change shadows into rainbows. We are creatures of dreaming. We lie on our backs as children and make pictures in the clouds. We imagine putting a man on the moon, and we do. And some of us envision healing ourselves, and we can.

The question may be whether or not grief needs to be healed, or if it only needs to be nursed into wellness. To say that grief needs to be healed suggests that there is damage that needs to be corrected, hopefully without leaving any scars. But when we're grieving, all we really want is a little nursing—a little tender loving care—a little chicken soup to comfort us, until the shadows pass and all that remains is the rainbow.

LOSS

When Jane was three years old her kitten died. Her parents told her it had "gone away."

When Dick was four years old, his mother died after a long illness at home. His father told him that, "God took Mommy."

These all too common explanations of death seem harmless enough, but they can be dangerous. What we tell children about death may effect how they deal with loss for the rest of their lives. By trying to spare them the pain of grief as children, we may actually cause them to suffer greater grief later in life.

The greatest single mistake we make with grieving children is to underestimate their ability to understand the truth about death. Children who are dying face death head-on, without evasion, avoidance, or sugar-coated illusions. Just the plain truth. They deal with death a hundred percent better than any adult around them. They yearn for their parents to face the reality of their impending death so that they can enjoy their remaining time together. Kids want their doctors and nurses and parents and friends to stop pretending that everything is OK when they know it isn't.

The simplicity of truth is essential to dealing with death—especially the death of a loved one. Simple expressions that we use without considering their impact may actually cause a child pain. "I'm sorry you lost your mother" may leave a child feeling responsible for a parent's death. But the mother isn't lost, she is dead, and the child had nothing to do with it.

When Jane was told that her kitten had *gone away* she may have been left with two incorrect impressions: First, that it might some day return, and second, that its leaving might have been her fault. Why did her kitten "go away?" Perhaps she didn't love it enough.

When people leave us, we all want and need to know the real reason why. Children need the truth so that they don't become confused about their responsibility in the event. When parents divorce, children often blame themselves for the failures of their parents. Death, like divorce, is a going-away process that confuses children.

A three-year-old may not understand the process of death, but will understand words such as, "Grandma died and won't be coming back to see us anymore. But she will always love you and you will always love and remember her, and she will live in your heart forever."

The loss of a pet can be just as devastating to a child as the loss of a relative, and it is important not to underestimate the sense of loss a child experiences. "Muffin has died and won't be back to play with you anymore. But you'll always remember how much she loved you and enjoyed playing with you, and you will always have those memories of her."

What comforts all of us in our loss is what I call the blessing of remembrance. After grief comes solace, the solace of remembering all that we enjoyed about our loved one. Children especially need that same solace.

Telling a child that "God took Mommy," can deprive a child of an important source of comfort. The child may ask why God took Mommy when the child needed her. The child may become angry or resentful of God. So if we choose to speak of God in terms of death, it might be better to say that, "Death took Mommy, and now she is with God." Now death, not God, is responsible for Mommy's going away, and the child can take comfort in the fact that Mommy is safe with God.

Children see and hear about death every day. Plants and flowers fade and die. Leaves wither and fall from the trees. Fairy tales and television shows are filled with stories of death. But when it really happens to children, they are just as unprepared as an adult. What was once an abstraction is now a harsh reality. To help them deal with that reality we must tell them the truth with compassion, and share our grief with them.

I once heard a little girl of seven who knew she was dying tell her mother, "It's OK to feel sad, Mommy—it's OK to cry."

The human spirit, like the human body, heals in its own time and in its own way.

FINDING THE WORDS

To most folks, I appear to be a rather pleasant older gentleman with a twinkle in my eye and a grin on my face. I'm told that I look like Kenny Rogers or maybe Santa Claus. Those guys are pretty nice-looking fellows, so I don't mind the comparison. Now, we all know that everyone has a dark side to their nature. But imagine my surprise when I learned that one of the women in a discussion group I was leading for widows had cautioned a newcomer that she shouldn't be, "fooled by that twinkle in his eye—he can be a really devious S.O.B."

Moi? Never! Well, hardly ever.

The reason for this caution came out of an experiment. I had been watching the late show on television one night—it was that old Joan Crawford/Betty Davis potboiler, *Whatever Happened to Baby Jane?* In the film, the young Baby Jane becomes famous singing a song about her father who has died. The lyrics to the song go: "I've written a letter to daddy—his address is heaven above."

That gave me an idea—I thought that everyone should write letters to their partners who were now at the "address above." It seemed like a good way to focus on some of their problems, their anger, their sense of loss, and their bewilderment.

Everyone wrote a letter, and a lot of good stuff came out of the experiment. Things that had gone unexpressed were said, and emotions ran pretty high. Then (and here's why I earned the reputation of being a devious S.O.B.), I asked them to answer their own letters. This was not easy for any of them. But in the end, after they had really struggled, the answers flowed.

We all shared our letters with one another, and we were all feeling our own pain, and each other's pain, and we cried and hugged and laughed and cried some more. We shed some anger. We shed some anxiety. We shed some sorrow. And we shed a lot of tears.

Of all the letters, two summed up what all of us believed in our hearts.

"Dear Stan, I miss you. Love, Laurie."

"Dear Laurie, I miss you, too. Love, Stan."

PART TWO:
Grieving

A Sock and a Shoe

Last summer, the Eggheads and I went for a weekend in the woods. The Eggheads are children who have lost their hair during chemotherapy. Many of them are in remission, but they are all classified as terminal.

This weekend was our chance to get away from the hospital and "let our hair down," as the joke went. We swam in the pool, hiked in the woods, and roasted marshmallows around the campfire. And just like *normal* campers, we sang songs and told ghost stories.

Sunday morning broke bright and sunny with the promise of perfect weather and a full day of outdoor pleasures—a rare treat for these kids who spend too many hours cooped-up indoors. As I entered the dorm where several young boys had slept, I found Seth and Ryan having a heated argument about the correct way to put on socks and shoes.

"A sock and a shoe," insisted Seth.

"Sock, sock, then shoe, shoe," yelled Ryan.

"Wait a minute!" I shouted over their ravings. "This is a silly discussion."

"Who are you calling silly, Mister Silly?" they

chimed in, attempting to put me in my place.

"OK, now listen to me, you guys. This discussion cannot continue because there is no right answer. It is a matter of personal choice, and there is no right or wrong way. Got it?"

They looked at me oddly, and I realized that I had spoiled their fun by acting like a grownup full of logic and reason.

"Tell you what, forget the argument and both wear sandals—or just go barefoot. OK?"

They both giggled and threw their pillows at me.

I remember a similar discussion in a college philosophy class. We were discussing the great theoretical debates of the Renaissance religious leaders about the number of angels who could dance on the head of a pin. Our professor had pointed out that it depended on how fat or thin each particular angel was.

"Always," he cautioned with an index finger lifted skyward, "Answer a ridiculous question with a ridiculous answer." I liked his wisdom.

Whenever I am tempted to give a single answer to any question, I am reminded of my professor's caution about absolute answers. A wise person knows that there is more than one path through the forest.

That's why when someone asks me a silly question, such as, "How long is too long to grieve?" or, "When will the pain stop?" I ask them if they put on a sock and a shoe, or a sock and a sock and then a shoe and a shoe.

Answering the All Aboard

In the train station of Life and Death we all have the same choices to make. When the train departs, taking our loved one away, we are left with only our grief and pain of loss.

When the "all aboard" for the train back to Life is called, we can choose to climb aboard, or to wait for the next train. The most comforting thing about these trains is that they are always departing, round the clock. So when you *are* ready to make the trip back to life, there is always a train waiting to take you there.

There was a time when I couldn't understand people who seemed able to get on with their lives after a loved one had died. I especially couldn't fathom the ones who did it quickly. How much could they really have loved, I'd think, if they were already back at work, eating out, and going on dates?

Later I realized that their timetables were just different from mine. They didn't love less or grieve less or honor less—they simply did it differently. True, some of them were in denial, just delaying the devastation of grief. But others were actually moving on—getting back into life. While it may not have been my way, it worked for them.

My grandmother amazed me when her lifelong friend and champion bridge partner died. "Well, who will I play cards with now that Vinnie has gone off and died?" she asked. I thought that comment lacked any sense of mourning for her dear departed cohort, and I told her so. I was twelve.

"Now you listen to me," she said gently as she pulled me down on the sofa beside her, "Vinnie heard the whistle blow and off she went. We knew that one of us would go first, and we made a deal to hold a place at the card table upstairs for the other. Now just because she got the call first is no reason to get all teary-eyed and sad. She's very likely better off than we are. I'll miss her, but things go on—and so will I.

"Now, are you going to learn to play bridge or am I

going to have to recruit one of those old biddies from the church?"

My grandmother was always "getting on with things," and death was no different from anything else. Nana Laura died a few years later at home after a long, painful battle with cancer. At the end she was still telling me to get on with things. After I took time to say goodbye and feel my loss, I did.

"Getting on with things" was one of the many beautiful gifts she left to me. That, and how to keep a poker-face during a bridge game.

HUGGING, HOLDING HANDS, AND HEALING

When confronted with death we are often rendered speechless. There seem to be no words to explain or to comfort.

The problem isn't so much that we don't know what to say. It's that we don't hear what we're being told. So instead of talking, we must learn to listen. And we must listen aggressively to understand. We must wipe our mind and our vision clean, so that we can see and hear everything without being interrupted or distracted by our own ideas and responses.

Since the words of the dying and the grieving are in a language basically foreign to our everyday language, we are faced with the difficulty of translating that language into our own. The dying and the grieving have their own words for their feelings, and we must listen carefully and completely to their exact wording in order to translate and understand.

The key to understanding language is realizing that all words have two meanings. "I love you," has one meaning to the person who says it and another to the person who hears it. This is equally true of gestures. Gestures are even less explicit than speech—they require facial accents to enhance their meaning and clarity. In some cases, body language completes the communication.

I began to realize that the meanings of words and gestures were not always clear and exact, and that they were often more crucial to the sender than the receiver. For example, when I approach a grieving person and say, "Would you like a hug?" and they respond that they would, I then ask, "A father hug? A friend hug? A lover hug?" The person may respond by choosing one of those or perhaps by requesting another type of hug. The hug I give is essentially the same each time—what's important about it is their response.

Touching and hand-holding provide a similar line of communication by a different route. Sitting and listening aggressively is good, but sometimes I wanted a quicker response. When trying to create a mental space for opening up and letting go, I found that the moment I made any kind of physical contact, the process sped up tenfold. Touching became a short cut—a sort of conversational shorthand.

With both dying and grieving, the process of "letting go" is essential. We can not move on to death or to life until we let go of fear and anxiety and anger and a host of other emotions that entrap us and hold us captive in an unresolved space. Simply suggesting that a person "let go" seemed to be unproductive, so I developed a strategy to break through the defensive line.

I ask the person to hold my fingertips with theirs and to release some of their grief (or fear or anger) into my fingertips, to pass that negative energy to me. But I ask them only to release as much as they are willing to give up at that moment. The release process seldom lasts more than a few seconds, but the effect is instantaneous and remarkable. The person experiences letting go, and for that moment understands that it is both a physical and a mental experience.

Communication is very often a hands-on experience, and not simply a matter of being a good aggressive listener. If one picture is worth a thousand words, how many thousands of words can be replaced by a gently held hand or a healing hug?

HARMONY

Here, take my hand. Let me guide you along the path. We'll talk together, gather wildflowers and share some memories. Hopefully, in time, the pain of your loss will lighten and you will begin the process of reentering life.

Just ahead is a road sign:

Welcome to Harmony

At first, Harmony was just a state of mind. It was a place I encouraged dying people to create in their consciousness where they could escape their fears of dying. It was simply a free-space, a kind of sanctuary. But then it became a reality. Sometimes a large room, or a wooded grove, or a rooftop in Manhattan would become the temporary location of Harmony.

In these spaces I sat with others in a circle, holding hands, breathing deeply, and sending ourselves to a place where everything was possible—a place where no questions went unanswered and no lies were told.

In the impossible world of death and dying, Harmony is a refuge. At first, only terminal patients went to Harmony—groups of children who needed to have a place where it was safe to speak the truth and to confront their anxieties. Later, older patients formed their own circles and traveled to Harmony in search of truth and release from fear.

Later still, circles of survivors formed: widows (both female and male), children whose parents, siblings, pets, and friends had died. All came to find—and to give—answers.

Each group taught me something new that I could share with the others. The widows formed what they called "the chain of life," in which each person pulled the next one a step closer to renewed life. The children began writing letters and tape-recording messages of truth for their parents: "Mommy, it's OK for you to cry;" "Daddy, stop pretending that I'm not dying."

And so, in time, The Harmony Project was born. Today, I still visit hospitals, but more and more I find myself sitting in a circle, and listening to questions and answers about death and dying and surviving.

The love and the wisdom in these circles humble me and fill me with wonder.

FIRST STEPS

As infants, we learn to walk by taking baby steps. Then we progress, our steps become bigger, more assured, until we are walking upright. Later, as children, we play a game in which we take baby steps or giant steps, forward or back. We've probably all heard the phrase, "May I take two giant steps?"

The journey out of grieving is like that game, because it too is made up of a series of steps: some large, some small, some forward—and some, from time to time, backward. What is important is not the direction of the movement, but the movement itself. Like all journeys, there are alternate paths to take. Some are more direct than others. Some more scenic. Others may be convoluted, even circuitous. But in the end, they all lead to the same destination.

When I am caught up in grief, when I cannot tell if I am taking baby steps forward or giant steps back, I listen to the children.

Every time I am perplexed by life—by unanswered prayers, by unsolved mysteries and quandary rather than clarity—the wisdom of children never ceases to amaze me.

One day I was sitting with a group of kids in a Harmony circle. We held hands, eyes closed, and thought about someone we loved who had died and gone away. When we were all breathing quietly, I asked,

"What are you feeling?"

"Frightened," answered Jenny, whose mother had died.

"Of what?"

"That my father will die too and leave me all alone."

"That could happen," I replied. "In fact, someday he will die—just like all of us will. But probably not for a long time from now. Let's think only about tomorrow, Jenny. Let's think about how wonderful tomorrow will be with your dad. Can you do that?"

"I'll try, but it won't be easy because . . . because I'm still afraid he'll die and leave me and then I'll be alone."

"That's how I felt when my sister died," said Andrea. "We were identical twins and I always felt as though we were two halves of the same coin. I mean we were so much a part of each other and now I feel that half of me is gone. That I am only half."

We sat for a few moments watching Jenny and Andrea as they considered their sadness and fear. I asked if anyone had an idea about what they might do to feel better. Bobby, age seven, had the answer.

"Andy, you said that you felt like you and your sister were two sides of a coin, and now that she's gone you feel as if half of you is gone. But that must mean that half of your sister is still here."

"What?" responded Andrea, a bit bewildered.

"If part of you is gone with her, then part of her stayed behind with you. Don't you get it? It works both ways."

We call that two-way process "memory." I believe that being forgotten is the only real death. Once we say goodbye, then we are able to journey back into life, fortified with our memories.

We may feel that half of us is gone, but we are comforted by the thought that half remains behind, in our hearts and memories.

And that is one giant step forward.

LETTERS OF LOVE

Sitting in a circle of children who have lost either a parent, both parents, a brother, or a sister, I see how frightened they are. Harmony is a new experience for them—a place where they are told they are safe. A place for telling the truth, and asking questions, and hearing answers. We hold hands, perhaps a bit too tightly, and breathe deeply in an attempt to relax.

After we have finished our breathing exercise I ask the first question, "What makes you angry about the death of your loved one?"

"The autopsy," respond several of the kids.

I was surprised by their response because it was the first time I had ever heard it.

"My sister was murdered. Why did they have to do an autopsy on her?"

I was tempted to give her the probable legal reason for an autopsy that seemed so blatantly unnecessary, but I resisted because I doubted that it would ease her pain.

"What else makes you angry?"

"The way they paint up dead people to make them look alive. They didn't even part my brother's hair right."

Again, several nods of agreement from the rest of the group.

"I don't want to remember my mommy in the coffin. Why did they make me look at her and touch her? She was so cold. My mommy wasn't cold."

"It's sick, man, the way they dress up the body and put makeup on it and then stick it in a coffin and make you pass by and say goodbye. It's sick!"

Everyone agrees. Their anger is focused on the body of their loved one, and on what they see as a violation of that body. They seem unable to get past their feelings of physical violation.

I remember a comment I once heard about the body in death and I share it with them. It might help.

"Imagine that your loved one who has died writes you a letter. Now in this letter they tell you every wonderful experience they had in their lifetime. They tell you all about themselves so that you really can remember them. Now, imagine that also in this letter they tell you how much they love you and how they understand how much you love and miss them. Wouldn't that be a wonderful letter to get?" They all agree that it would be.

"Imagine opening up your mailbox and finding that wonderful letter inside. You'd open the envelope and take out the letter and read the precious words that would make you so happy—Now, what about the envelope?"

They all looked at me, not understanding.

"Well, now you have this wonderful letter that came inside an envelope. So, what about the envelope? How important is the envelope? Is it OK to throw it away?"

"Sure," they respond.

"Well, the body we live in is like the envelope. The letter is who we are, what we think and feel, and that's the most important thing there is. It's OK to throw the envelope away—to bury it, because we always have the letter.

"The letter is our memory of the person we love who has died. So it's all right to let go of the envelope, because we have the letter."

"What about the stamp?" Susan asks.

"The stamp?" I reply, puzzled.

"Well, stamps can be valuable. Can we keep the stamp?"

"What do you think the stamp on this envelope looks like?"

"I think it's a picture of the person who wrote the letter."

Just when I think I'm enlightening them they enlighten me. I think of my own personal album, filled with the stamps of those I love who have given me the letters of their life and love. Like rare stamps beyond price, they gaze back at me and remind me again and again of a time that was and is no more.

And from time to time I reread those letters, and relive those precious moments, and I touch the photo-stamps—and I am blessed with remembrance.

REMEMBRANCE

If we are loved and remembered, then we live on for-ever in the hearts of those who love us. This thought comforts me—and I find it equally sustaining when I remember a loved one who has died. I am saddened that I will never see that person again, but I am comforted by the great wealth of memories and love that are stored in my heart and mind.

When we grieve, we express our own sense of loss as well as the loss we perceive our loved one has suffered— the loss of life. And we deal with this double sense of loss separately.

Those who believe in an afterlife can take some

consolation in the belief that their loved one lives on in heaven. Those who believe in rebirth or reincarnation can take consolation that their loved one is merely in transition and will be reborn. Those who view death as a final exit, with nothing beyond, can take consolation that their loved one has completed life and is finally at rest. Ultimately, everyone wishes to believe that while they are suffering the loss of their loved one, that loved one is at peace, and in some form of grace.

These are important beliefs, for only after we have consoled ourselves with the idea that our loved one is safe and at peace can we begin to deal with *our* sense of loss.

I believe that the process of grief is different for each person, and that there are no rules of behavior, no specific, all-purpose processes that can provide easy answers to what may be unanswerable questions.

I don't believe that there is any time limit on how long a person should grieve. And I don't believe that there is any specific way in which they should stop grieving. Perhaps, as many people suggest, we never really stop grieving. Perhaps the feeling of loss stays with us until the end of our own lives.

I believe that the sense of loss continues forever, but I prefer to use that loss to honor and remember, not to be held in the grip of disabling sorrow and pain. What, I ask myself, would my loved one have wanted me to do with the rest of my life? Certainly not be consumed by grief. I believe that by living my life to its full potential I am honoring all that my partner expected from me—hoped and dreamed for me—in life. Still, for many the idea of reentering life without husband, or wife, or lover, or child, or sister, or brother is unimaginable.

Some surveys indicate that as a nation we have little or no patience with grieving people. When asked how long a person should grieve, most people answered, "A few weeks." Very few people considered anything longer either healthy or reasonable. My guess is that many of the people polled had never suffered the loss of a loved one. I know adults who openly acknowledge the grief they still feel over the childhood loss of a brother or sister. Old men and women still grieve for parents long departed.

Like death itself, grief is best managed by facing it straight on.

"I am overwhelmed with grief," is a statement that reveals a person faced with a sadness so encompassing that it consumes them. "I am paralyzed with fear," reveals a fear so numbing that it renders the person immobile.

"I feel crushed by my pain," describes a weight so great that the person is buried beneath it. None of these images is manageable.

When people with these feelings come to me for help, I begin by suggesting that they change their description to something less intimidating.

"Overwhelmed" is such a large concept that there is no way over or around it. One pictures a huge obstacle sitting in the pathway back to life. So we must dismantle that object and reduce it to smaller, more manageable parts. We must break it down to smaller pieces.

This process can be accomplished by determining where and when the sense of being overwhelmed is most intense. Some questions that help to do this are:

"What time of day do I feel it most or least?"

"Do I feel it more or less when I am alone?"

"Do friends and family intensify or relieve the feeling? How about children? Co-workers? Neighbors?"

Each question and each answer will whittle down the size and shape of the overwhelming grief. After a couple of rounds of twenty questions, you may see a new and much clearer picture of your overwhelming grief.

Perhaps the questioning will reveal that you feel your most intense feelings primarily in the morning. That might make you anxious about going out or having anyone in to visit. So stay home by yourself and indulge your grief with memories of your loved one until your grief is balanced with the sense of shared happiness a positive memory brings. Being told to "put it out of your mind," is bad advice. Remembering can be a joy when you are grieving. It brings your loved one back into your life.

Or perhaps you'll discover that being alone intensifies your grief, but that friends and family also intensify the feeling. If that happens, go out to the mall or the park and spend time among strangers. Have a casual conversation with someone or find a diverting activity that requires nonpersonal interaction. Go to a movie or a video arcade and play a game. Join a gym or take a dance class.

These distractions are not solutions, but they are ways to divert overwhelming grief for a period of time—a kind of breathing space, or stress reduction. (Keep in mind that we are not trying to change the intensity of the grief, just the perception that it is overwhelming, and therefore unmanageable.)

As you ask and answer each question, and the true shape of your grief becomes visible, you will see that the unknown is more formidable than the known. The shapeless night is more terrifying than the visible day.

By making death and grieving visible in daylight we can manage it much better.

Throughout all of this, your memories will sustain you—they are the reality of your love. They are the guide that will lead you home through the blackness of night and the swirling fog of obscurity. Once home, your memories will surround and comfort you.

Do we ever stop grieving? Probably not—we just call it something else. We call it honoring and remembering.

PART THREE:
At Sea

LIFE IS A BOAT

There's a terrible old joke about a man who seeks the answer to the age-old question, "What is life?" The man questions every religion, every philosophy, and none provides him with a satisfying answer. Finally, in desperation, he climbs the cliffs of the Himalayas, searching for an ancient guru who is reported to have *the answer*. He finds the wizened one perched on a rock overlooking the vast world below him, and he poses the question.

"What is life?"

"Life," responds the guru, "is a boat."

"Life is a boat?" asks the man incredulously.

"Life isn't a boat?" says the guru.

• • •

OK, it's a bad joke, but it makes a good point. No one has an absolute answer to anything.

However, for our purposes, life *is* a boat. Life may be an expensive yacht, a speedboat, a sailboat, or a row-boat—for each vessel, in its own way, is a pleasure craft, and might even get us where we want to go. But, life is also a sea, and we must navigate carefully.

If we look at a loved one's death as a storm on the sea of life, then we can examine how our individual craft might weather that storm and its aftermath.

And that's what we'll look at in the chapters ahead.

ADRIFT

One of my favorite stories was *Swiss Family Robinson*, the tale of a family of castaways who, after their ship sinks, find a new life on an island paradise.

The death of someone we love often sets us adrift, without anchor or direction. Our little boat is tossed about on the sea of grief, and we feel powerless to do anything but ride out the storm. This wait-and-see plan often appears to be the only solution.

"When my husband died I didn't know what to do."

"I felt the same way when John passed away. I had depended on him for everything, and then suddenly I was alone and had to fend for myself. I tell you, it wasn't easy."

"After Bobby died, I wandered around the neighborhood visiting my friends, sitting motionless in their kitchens, drinking endless cups of coffee—listening but not hearing what they were saying."

"You'd think that a woman like me who had worked all her life in a responsible position would be able to handle the death of her husband. Ha! Guess again. I completely fell apart. I used to kid Sam that if I died, he'd starve to death because he couldn't find his socks, and so he couldn't finish dressing. Naturally, he couldn't go out to eat, so he'd starve to death. Well, let me tell you—that was me. I started out of the house one morning in a navy suit and pink satin bedroom slippers. . . . It wasn't as funny then as it seems now."

"That's the truth. I couldn't even get dressed in the morning. I'd get up, make coffee, turn on the TV, and suddenly my kids were home from school and I was still in my housecoat. I don't know where the hours went or what I did."

Adrift. Wandering around. Lost in grieving. Not letting go, but being cut loose. A castaway is a person set adrift or one whose boat has been cut from its anchor.

Like the Robinson family, some people—in time, and due to good winds and favorable currents—may land on the shore of a new life, an island paradise. But others may remain directionless, with no safe harbor on the horizon.

BECALMED

A ship floats still on a dead sea. Overhead, the blazing, relentless sun drains moisture from the plate-glass surface of the water. The tiny craft of life rocks back and forth, making no headway. Time and life are at a standstill.

• • •

Steve and Joanna had been divorced three months when Joanna was killed in a car crash. Their marriage, the result of a passionate, whirlwind courtship, had diminished into a routine coupling that left both of them angry and yearning. Finally, unable to recapture their passion, they separated and divorced. What remained in their hearts and minds were the memories of their youthful romance. The thousand tiny indignities of daily life that had driven them apart were soon forgotten.

They both carried the burden of remorse for what they had lost, and bewilderment about why it had happened. They tried to reconcile, but each time the romance was shattered by the same harsh realities that had originally driven them apart. The old wounds were reopened and unhealed.

When Joanna was killed, Steve was stunned. Like many men, Steve couldn't cry. He withdrew into himself and layered one grief on top of another. His memories offered not consolation but indictment. Acting as judge and jury, he convicted himself of having caused the death of his marriage and the death of his wife. If he hadn't left her, he reasoned, she would still be alive.

Days turned into weeks and then months. His grief, intensified by his guilt, took its toll on his work and health. He was plagued by nightmares. His waking hours were consumed by damning thoughts that all began with the phrase, "If I hadn't . . ." and ended with the phrase, ". . . she would be alive today." Never did Steve entertain the thought that the accident might have happened even if they were still happily married. He couldn't accept that idea—an idea that might have gotten him off the hook of his guilt and forced him to deal with his pain.

Steve was hung up on his grief and on his guilt. He was *hooked* on it—like an addict is hooked on drugs. Steve was becoming a guilt-and-grief junkie, and it had brought his craft of life to a standstill.

Just as there are twelve-step programs for more common addictions, there are programs for people addicted to their grief. These programs all have the same basic purpose—to get an individual to let go of the addiction and to reenter life. We describe this process of letting go and moving forward as getting clean. When a junkie kicks his habit, he is clean.

The phrase "kick the habit" gives us a clear image of just how active and involved we must be to overcome addiction. We must give that habit a good, swift kick in the pants—we must boot it out of our lives. Often, the results of a twelve-step program are described as a turn-around. This means a complete 360-degree turn—which brings us right back to where we started. So the cleansing is in the turning. It is the process of turning around that creates the change. This is not a matter of finding a new direction after a mere 90- or 180-degree turn, but of coming back to where you started and continuing your life from where you left off.

Steve resisted joining one of the widow's groups. He sat in on a couple of sessions and decided that his problem ran much deeper than anyone else's. To him it was more than paralyzing grief that kept his life in suspension. He was still too guilty to grieve.

"It isn't the idea that most of the people in the group are women," he explained. "But most of them have found a way to cry, and the few who haven't gotten that far at least *feel* they can get there. I don't even feel that."

"What do you feel, Steve?"

"That I killed Joanna. That if I'd stayed in the marriage this wouldn't have happened."

"But you know that isn't true, don't you?"

"Sure, intellectually I do, but I feel responsible anyway. I feel guilty because—because I left her."

"Did you leave her? I thought you had left each other."

"I still feel responsible because I couldn't give her what she wanted and needed, so it's my fault."

"Did Joanna give you what you wanted and needed?"

"No—not always, but she tried to."

"And you tried to give her what she wanted and needed, too."

"Yes, but it's not the same thing."

"Why?" I asked, wondering what he was thinking.

"Because now she's dead."

"No second chance to forgive you—is that it?"

Steve glared at me before he nodded yes, and looked away, still unable to accept the truth.

In Harmony there is a group of fathers whose sons were homosexual and who died of AIDS. The pain and grief of these fathers, like Steve's, is filled with remorse and guilt. Many of them refused to visit their dying sons in their hospital beds. They sat, stone-faced with rage, chain-smoking in hospital waiting rooms while their wives sat alone with their dying sons.

Afterward, nightmares began to plague them. Their unwept tears were like knives in their hearts. Haunted now by memories of their sons as children—innocent and loving, rushing to greet Daddy, happy to be in his arms, delighted to be called son—these fathers became desolate and becalmed in grief and guilt.

Even those who had achieved some form of last-minute closing were trapped in unforgiving guilt. Yes, they had embraced their sons, spoken the words "I love you," and watched their sons slip away—but they had not forgiven them for being gay. Now, they too carried the burden of guilt that kept them from grieving, from letting go, from healing—from moving forward to honoring and remembering. Their memories didn't comfort, but like Steve's, indicted them and found them guilty.

As part of the healing and forgiving process, these fathers make quilt panels honoring their sons. These quilts are sent to The Names Project, where they are joined with thousands of others honoring men, women, and children who have died of AIDS.

It was here, among these struggling men, that Steve found his way. He realized that he and Joanna had never really stopped loving each other—they had simply moved apart.

Sitting cross-legged on the floor, cutting pieces of bright fabric to make a memorial of his own for Joanna, he finally and completely accepted the truth about what had happened to them. He found his cleansing, his turn-around, and, eventually, his tears.

UNDERTOW

As a child, I was fascinated and delighted by the ocean. Most summers my family rented a cottage on the beach at the tip of Long Island. Every bright morning I'd dash out of our cottage and dance among the seashells and the crashing surf. Long before I could swim, I'd leap into the waves and enjoy the rush of foam that splashed around me. Sometimes the waves would knock me down, filling my mouth with salty sea water, but I'd resurface, laughing, and once again let the ocean pound against me. People commented that I was fearless. My father replied that I was just too dumb to know better.

But I did know about one thing—the undertow. Dad made sure of that. Carefully and precisely my father described the subtle, invisible force that hid beneath even the calmest sea: swift, strong currents that could drag even the strongest swimmer away from the safety of the beach, sweep him out to sea, and drown him.

This was no idle fairy tale or horror story—I actually saw it happen when I was seven years old. I stood beside my father and dozens of swimmers, and we saw a man swept away and sucked under, saw the lifeguards desperately try to reach him, risking their own lives in the attempt. But it all happened so quickly. The force of the undertow was too great.

What is most treacherous about the undertow is that it runs so close to the shore. When we survivors struggle toward the new shore of life we must be aware that danger still lurks below the surface, just a few yards from apparent safety.

Grief has its own undertow, an undertow that can be just as treacherous as the one beneath the sea. As we let go of grief and move once again toward a new life, we often misjudge our strength and readiness. As survivors, we want to move forward. We want the blessing of honoring and remembrance, and we want to get back into life again. But we aren't always ready.

• • •

"When Becky died, I thought that I'd never have another happy day. But time seemed to ease the pain and I thought that I was really getting a handle on it. When spring came, and there was all that rebirth around me, I thought that I was having a rebirth too. I let myself enjoy life and i even started letting myself enjoy memories of her that had been too painful before. They seemed not to be now.

"At the end of June we had the memorial service, and placed her headstone. Everything went fine and beautifully, and the families seemed to be drawn closer in that moment—strengthened almost—by our mutual loss.

"We were walking back to our cars, and I turned to look at Becky's headstone one more time. And WHAM! It hit me like a punch in the gut. 'She's really gone.' And out of nowhere the pain overwhelmed me."

• • •

It is not without reason that the widows of Harmony refer to their healing process as a lifeline. As members of the group gain insight into their grief and share that knowledge with the group, we say that they have "moved forward." From week to week, the balance changes, depending upon how each member gains strength.

At the end of each session, we all have a sense of who has moved forward and who has not. We form a chain. We hold hands, and the stronger people in the chain (the people closer to the front) reach back to pull the next person forward, in a symbolic gesture of rescue.

Those who have reached the shore turn and pull the others out of the crashing surf of their grief, saving them from being pulled down by the undertow.

SCUTTLED

Sometimes, people sabotage their own best efforts— they "scuttle" their own lifeboats.

When someone we love dies, each of us reacts differently. Just as there is no one perfect way to say goodbye, there is no one perfect way to let go and move ahead to a new life. How much easier it would be if there were—we all prefer easy answers.

There are times when grief continually scuttles our efforts to survive and reach the new shore. Again and again the rescue efforts of well-meaning friends and counselors are thwarted by holes we punch in the lifeboat. The would-be survivor becomes her own worst enemy, and once again she is plunged into a sea of grief that threatens to drown her.

Some of these struggling survivors will, in their own time, find a new safe harbor. But many will need to be rescued from themselves.

The death of a loved one sometimes brings on thoughts of suicide. I have often seen one partner follow the other in death soon after the first person's passing—for no apparent reason other than a broken heart.

While we cannot, and should not, try to keep anyone from grieving, we must be alert to signals that indicate they may be about to scuttle their own boat of life. Dozens of wonderful books have been written about the tragedy of suicide and how to cope with the warning signs. But our individuality renders all of that information hypothetical—they are a series of fine but imperfect guidelines.

Listen to the words of grieving friends and loved

ones—the words that may show they are scuttling their survival. Even a person in the deepest despair of grief will speak of things in positive terms. But the potential suicide, the person who wills himself toward death, will express that desire in more subtle negative ways.

We must, once again, become aggressive listeners. We must clear away our own thoughts so that we can really hear what we're being told. Almost always, those who seem to be scuttling are reaching out for help, looking for a lifeline. We must hear their cries. For we are all survivors—but some of us need to be rescued now and then.

Sink or Swim

Recently, I was invited to speak at a national conference on grief. The audience comprised professional caregivers: doctors, nurses, therapists, counselors, clergy, and an assortment of workers in related areas. I had never attended a conference like this and had no idea what to expect.

One of the other speakers, a well-known, highly-respected, best-selling author, had recently suffered a great personal loss. As she approached the podium, I was struck by her appearance and body language. Clearly, she was still in the depths of grief. Just moving seemed to be a struggle for her.

She gripped the sides of the podium and faced her audience. Her speech focused on her sudden loss, and how it had changed her life. Within moments she was in the grips of reawakened grief, and she pelted the audience with fiery balls of rage and agonized bewilderment, as well as the categorical denouncement of every known solace. Some people, myself included, were simply stunned. Others rose and left the room.

As she raged on, she demanded sympathy and empathy from her audience, and accused them of failure when they were unable to give it. I wondered where all this was leading. Perhaps, I speculated, she is running her boat head-on toward the rocks, and now she will show us how, with strength and ingenuity, to maneuver her imperiled craft to a safe harbor.

Instead, right before our eyes, she sped on and dashed herself on the rocks. At the end of her speech, she was a spent, smoldering pile of charred remains. I was shocked—totally confused as to the reason and value in such a performance.

• • •

Later, still haunted by the spectacle of her grief, I re-
called a moment from one of my Harmony sessions. One
of the members of the group was sharing a painful experience. Like the speaker at the conference, he heaped his
grief upon us until we were all reeling with him in his
pain. We offered as much comfort and support as human-
ly possible—but our support was but a drop of rain on
raging fire—almost worthless.

Afterward, another member of the group who knew
about a loss I had experienced that was almost identical to
the speaker's, challenged me to explain why I hadn't
shared that fact with this grieving person. I responded,

"Showing him my wounds would not stop his bleeding."

One of the strengths and weaknesses of all groups
(including twelve-step programs) is the belief that misery
loves company. Perhaps. But the nature of that company
makes a difference. A support group should do just that—
support.

Support comes in a variety of forms. Hugging someone—comforting them, soothing their pain—is a form of
support. So is cheering on someone who is about to
make a breakthrough. And so is a no-nonsense, straight-
truth approach.

Jesus didn't pick up and carry the people he healed. He told them to throw away their crutches and walk on their own. To support someone's desire to stand up and walk is one thing. To become their crutch is quite another.

While at one time it might have been of value to tell that man that I had suffered a similar loss and had moved on to find the gift of remembrance, this was not that time. This man was still in the grip of despair, hopelessly lost at sea. What he needed was a compassionate guide, not the affront of someone who had overcome the same challenge. It is no comfort to be reminded that others have accomplished what you are unable to.

There is nothing more offensive than the presumptuous phrase, "I know how you feel."

No, you don't!

Two people standing in the rain both get wet. But they experience that wetness differently. They can share an umbrella. They can share their discomfort. But the actual experience will be different for both. No amount of empathy or sympathy will ever allow one of them to presume understanding the other.

The expression, "You can't understand a man until you walk a mile in his shoes," is for me a total fraud. All you learn from that is the relative size of your feet. If you *really* want to understand a man, walk a mile beside him. Keep silent. Listen to what he tells you. You can't wear his shoes, but you can learn how they feel on his feet.

• • •

I sat stunned in that auditorium after the speaker had descended from the stage and the audience had filed out in a variety of moods. I wondered what I might think later on, after I had had time to digest it all. Was there, I wondered, some good to be found among the ashes and debris?

In time, I saw there was. The lesson was this: If your life's craft seems headed for the rocks, it is up to you to seize the wheel and try for a safe port. If you don't, you may crash and burn.

Sink or swim—it's that simple.

LIFEBOAT

As a youth, I loved seafaring adventure films. I'd sit on the edge of my seat in the darkened theater as sailors tried in vain to save the sail or dodge the falling mast. When the ship finally succumbed to the torrents of the sea and sank majestically to the depths below, I breathed a sigh of relief as the tiny lifeboats carried the passengers away from death. To me, the sea became a metaphor for all calamity—even death.

Of all maritime disasters, the most famous is the sinking of the *Titanic*. Dozens of films have been made about this event, and dozens more have been inspired by the stories of people aboard that ill-fated vessel.

My favorite of those films is the 1964 Debbie Reynolds musical, *The Unsinkable Molly Brown*. Loosely based on the true story of a woman who survived the sinking of the *Titanic*, the story is mainly about someone who couldn't be held down. Throughout this rags-to-riches story, Molly is a supreme survivor. She overcomes one adversity after another. When the *Titanic* sinks under her, she jumps in a lifeboat and challenges all aboard to row for their lives. She takes charge of her life and faces adversity head on with her famous battle cry, "I ain't down yet!"

Like Molly, when our life ship is destroyed by the sea, we must climb into a lifeboat and become a survivor. We must grab a life preserver, or a bit of floating debris that will carry us to safety. Some of us need to be rescued. But others are strong swimmers who are determined to reach shore again. Survive we must, no matter what.

The *Titanic* was not unsinkable, as man, in his profound arrogance, once claimed. Nor are people. But although the ship of life may be struck by the giant iceberg of death and grief, it is the human heart and spirit that become the lifeboat that keeps us afloat.

The ship may go down. But we ain't down yet.

MANEUVERING

Sometimes, even after finding a lifeboat, we must maneuver to avoid the dangerous debris that is left in the aftermath of tragedy. Just climbing into a lifeboat is not enough to bring us safely back to land—we must traverse additional dangers by strategic patterns of movement and skillful changes of direction. Moving straight forward may not be the answer. Sometimes, only, zigzagging brings us safely ashore.

The sea of grief is particularly treacherous. It can be still one moment, and turbulent the next. One minute our craft of safety is bobbing quietly along, making headway under a gentle breeze. The next moment, it may be swamped under a pounding, crashing sea of angry waves.

• • •

"I just can't manage my mood swings," explained Janet with exhaustion in her voice. "Up one day and down the next. I have become what I never was before, a moody, oversensitive, manic-depressive, and I hate it. My kids don't know from one minute to the next if I'm going to be loving mommy or the Wicked Witch of the West."

"I know exactly what you mean," remarked Anita, who had been a widow for less than a month. "I was always stoic, even-tempered—now I fly off the handle at the slightest thing. I'm always on edge—raw, and easily provoked. I feel like I have 24-hour, 365-day PMS!"

Everyone chuckled at what was not a laughing matter. Grief changes us, and not always for the better. The romantic notions that pain purifies or that overcoming pain strengthens are difficult concepts to accept in the face of grief. Whether we are six years old and our kitten has died, or 65 and our life companion has died, the pain reshapes us.

We will always remain scarred, but we do not have to be disfigured.

When well-meaning people tell us to "get over" our loss, they are not only being unkind—they're also being stupid. None of us ever gets over the loss of a loved one. We survive it. And being a survivor is a lifelong venture.

The only way to survive the sea of grief is to learn to maneuver through its choppy waters. Mood swings are normal, just as the lack of mood swings is normal. "Normal" is what happens to you, not a standard imposed on you by self-styled well-meaning people.

Janet, whose mood swings turned her life into a see-saw, is a survivor. So are her children. But they are not in the same lifeboat. Each person has his or her own craft, and each must learn to maneuver independently—sometimes around one another. A sea full of debris can sink a lifeboat, and other survivors may crash into you in an attempt to save themselves.

Janet and her family must avoid damaging one another as they traverse the individual perils that face them. For while Janet is in rough seas, her children may be becalmed, or gently drifting, or already ashore. Where grief is concerned, we are not all in the same boat.

When an entire family suffers the same loss, there is some comfort in common grief. But all too often that grief creates more problems than it solves. Each member moves forward at a different pace, and some family members may fear and resent another's progress. We must be very careful not to impose our strategies for survival on others around us. We must grant everyone the same kindness and understanding that we expect from them.

So, as we zigzag our way to the shore, we may feel isolated even from those we usually feel closest to. When this happens it is best to remember that as survivors our goal is to be reunited safely on the shore. How we get there is not all that important. There are many different ways to maneuver in a choppy sea.

PILOTING

When a steamship enters the harbor and seeks to dock, they call for a *pilot* to come aboard and steer the vessel to port.

If our lifeboat is floundering offshore, we must sometimes enlist outside assistance to help us find safe haven. Therapists and counselors are the pilots who help us find our way and gently guide us back to shore. Not everyone has the skill and the stamina to fight the sea of grief alone. The size of our grief can overwhelm us and become unmanageable—and that's when we need a little outside help.

We have all seen pictures of beautiful luxury liners steaming into New York harbor. They are splendid, gleaming, smooth, and self-sufficient—until they get close to land. Then tiny little tugboats come alongside and gently nudge them toward the dock. These tiny boats ease them in the right direction so that their docking is safe and secure.

These ships are no less magnificent because they accepted help from a friendly little tugboat. We are no less magnificent if we, too, accept a helping hand.

SALVAGE

When our boat of life is tossed about in a storm of death, and the pressure from the pounding waves of grief causes us to feel as if we are breaking apart, we may feel that all is lost as our once-secure vessel (and our once-secure life) sinks beneath the sea.

But all is not lost. When a giant ship carrying precious cargo is torn apart and sunk at sea, divers eventually go down to retrieve that cargo. In maritime parlance, this is called *salvage*.

Alone and bewildered, numbed by sorrow, unable to envision life without the one we love, we often forget *our* precious cargo—our memories. When this happens, we too must mount a salvage operation. If the conditions are favorable, we may be able to recover what we've lost within a short time after the disaster. But this is not always possible.

Grief has its own set of seasons and its own time frame, which are different for each person. For this reason, the salvage operation may be delayed several months—even years.

For many people, memories are comforting and empowering. They move us forward. We use memories to enrich our lives and to honor the ones we love. They ease our pain and support us in our new lives.

But for others, memories can be as painful as the loss itself. In these cases, memories reinforce the feelings of loss and are not yet a comfort, not a part of life alone.

When the long winter of grief finally ends and spring begins, with its rebirth and awakening, memories, like tiny crocuses, bloom all around us.

I once visited a museum in Florida with an exhibition of artifacts retrieved from a sunken Spanish galleon. All of its precious gold coins were intact—as perfect and shiny as when they were made.

The same is true of our own golden memories. No matter how many seasons of grieving pass—no matter how many weeks or months or years go by—when the time comes for us to salvage them they will be as precious and perfect as the day they were created.

LAND HO

When Dorothy survives the tornado that twists, turns, and transports Auntie Em's house, she steps out into the Land of Oz and remarks to Toto, "I have a feeling we're not in Kansas anymore."

Any widow will tell you how strange the house she calls home looks, feels, and smells when she is there alone. Children who have lost a pet say their room feels empty. Brothers and sisters who have lost a sibling report that their rooms feel different—quiet. A now-single lover thrashes about, restlessly, in a half-empty bed.

When someone we love dies, a part of us is gone. We will never, ever, be the same.

As survivors, we must adjust to the new world just as the members of the Swiss Family Robinson had to. We make do. We jerry-rig everything because nothing is as it was before.

But if we have reached shore successfully, we are survivors and we are on solid ground again—no longer becalmed or adrift, no longer tossed about or swamped, no longer needing a pilot. We can begin to rebuild.

The Swiss Family Robinson built a new home from the wreckage of their ship. There, the children grew up and the family prospered, in a new way and in a new place.

As we survive and recover from the ordeal of grief we may find new life in the experience. We can, with strength and determination, rebuild our lives from the wreckage of death.

As we enter the period of reconstruction we do best when that reassembly is made up of positive, useful pieces of our former life salvaged from the time before the tornado of death shook us from our foundation and hurled us into a foreign land.

PART FOUR:
Coming Ashore

TIME OUT

All too often we find ourselves trying to help one another with a "One Size Fits All" approach—an off-the-rack, ready-to-wear set of solutions to what are really very personal and individual problems.

Remembering that the glass slipper only fits one foot, I offer this suggestion with a bit of hesitation. This is not for everyone.

When the going gets rough, when a new strategy is needed, when our burden is too heavy, we sometimes have to take a pause and call, "Time out."

Those who are in need of something invent a number of ways to satisfy that need. The need to find a way to deal with unmanageable grief led to the concept and the phrase "grief management."

Frankly, I don't think about managing grief unless it becomes disabling and dangerous. I tend to encourage full-out, no-holds-barred wailing, with garments rent and tears flowing like Niagara Falls. I believe in full indulgence of sorrow, because it speaks the truth of loss. To deny the loss, the tears, the despair, and the bewilderment of grief is to deny the love that makes that pain so great.

Only by giving full value to the pain of loss can one give full value to love.

Only then can we appreciate the full value of our memories and our consolation. Grieving and remembrance are our return on the investment of love. So just let the tears flow, and reach for another tissue.

But sometimes grief doesn't play fair. When it begins to hit us below the belt, and we are doubled over and disabled, it's time to blow the whistle.

Take a deep breath and get out of the game for a while. Now is the time to say you've had enough and you need a break. Now is the time to take a vacation.

I'm not suggesting that you simply put grief aside and walk away—that isn't possible. But you can stop for a moment and gather your resources before the next round.

If your helpful friends and family aren't helping, or if your support group isn't making you feel supported, then maybe you need to get away—away from what is too familiar and too painful: The empty house. The empty nursery. The empty kitchen. The empty workshop. The empty bed.

Now is the time to pack up and go away. Make no mistake, your grief will be your traveling companion—but new surroundings can change how things look and feel.

Just pick up and remove yourself from everything familiar. Everything that reminds you of your loss.

Grief is a mind, body, soul, and spirit experience— just like love. And if the experience is overwhelming you, maybe you should take your body away.

If you change your body's location, if you place it in totally new surroundings, then your thoughts and feelings will be forced to deal with the new surroundings, too. These changes will, in time, affect your spirit and soul. There is a temptation to call this a healing experience, but it is only a band-aid, a quick fix. It stops the bleeding— but the wound will take longer to heal.

The death of a loved one leaves us with a permanent scar. When I speak of healing, I am only talking about the open wound. Grief is the first stage of the healing process, the stage that enables us to release our pain and then, in time, find the final healing of remembrance.

THE MEASURE OF GRIEF

Amy and Brad had four children. Two of their sons died—one in a car accident at the age of twelve, the other in a miscarriage. Amy and Brad fully experienced the loss of both children, even though one of those children had never been born.

I was counseling their two surviving children, and I asked them about their loss. They responded that they had lost only one brother. They had experienced only the loss of the brother who had been born, who they knew and loved. Even though the miscarriage occurred during their lifetimes, they did not count that as a loss because, they said, "We never knew him."

But Amy and Brad experienced the death of their unborn child with the same pain as the loss of their living son. I realized that they had known that child in a way their children had not. The child in Amy's womb was *theirs*. They had created his life. They had hopes and dreams for him. From the moment of conception that baby existed for them, in their minds. He was already born, already living and breathing, already in Little League, already graduating from college, already married and producing the next generation of their family.

To the parents, the baby who died inside Amy's womb was not just a fetus that failed to come to full term, but a child with a complete life ahead of him. When that child died, his parents not only experienced the loss of a life that never was, but also the loss of a life that might have been. They had lost both their baby and their dreams.

I was reminded of something I read in an old Western novel when I was a boy. A pioneer woman, telling the story of her life, said, "I lost my firstborn in my sixth month." That unborn child would always be her "first-born" even though it never went to term, and no matter how many children she gave life to after that, she would always experience the loss of her firstborn.

The greatest error in judgment any of us can make is to try to measure grief and loss. We cannot know the depth of grief a mother feels over the loss of an unborn child, or how long she will mourn that loss any more than we can know the loss a child experiences when a pet dies.

We can never really know how another's grief feels. But we can be compassionate. We can put aside our own feelings and opinions, and trust their grief.

THE SEASON OF GRIEF

"For everything, there is a season," a familiar verse tells us.

Life and death come quickly in nature—buds swell into green leaves, turn golden, then brown, and drop to the earth. Nature shows us reincarnation as plants are reborn and flowers, once fresh with life, return to the earth to become nourishment for other plants.

Nature shows us seasons of life and death everywhere we look. But nature seems not to mourn these deaths—not the flowers, not even the animals. Within the life cycle is a built-in process of survival as one part of nature nourishes another.

But people do mourn and grieve—and so we alone need a season of grief. In this season, the seeds of rebirth are planted. What varies from person to person is the length of this season, the right time for harvest, and the time when rebirth comes.

When the seed of life is implanted in a woman we speak about her pregnancy going "full term." By this we mean that she will carry her unborn child the full term of nine months, without intervention. The season of grief must also be allowed, without intervention, to go to full term.

It makes me angry when people say, "Get on with your life, it's time to stop grieving." Nobody can tell you what the season of your grief is. It may be a summer, a

winter, a spring, a fall, perhaps another winter—or another—or another.

Just as the gestation period varies from creature to
creature, the natural process of grieving varies from person to person. The harvest of renewed life will come in its
own season.

PERMISSION TO GRIEVE

I am often stunned by the selfish tyranny of so-called
friends and loved ones who apply their standards for
grieving to someone else. The arrogant and thoughtless
attitude that they know when it's right to end grieving is
like a knife through an already-damaged heart.

• • •

Dan's marriage was shaky at best. When his mother
died, he felt more alone and isolated than ever. His family
seemed to be dealing with their loss better than he was,
and he looked to his wife for support. Her cold response
dismayed him. He decided that he wanted to get away
and give full vent to his grief. Tears had, so far, eluded

him, and he longed for the release they could provide.

He had always been the rock that his family's grief crashed against, and now he fulfilled that role again—even though he was the baby in the family, with his own needs. Dan decided to go to the beach for a few days, to have a remembrance closing with his mother. He wanted to be alone with her, walk and talk with her as they had so often when she was alive.

When he told his wife of his plan she responded in anger.

"Don't be ridiculous, Dan. Your mother is dead and gone and it's time to move on. I'm here and alive and I need you. No, absolutely no, you can't go."

So Dan didn't go.

During the weeks that followed, Dan never found his tears. Slowly, day by day, his wife displeased him more and more. After five months he divorced her.

Dan's story makes an important point. We do not need (or want) anyone else's permission to grieve. We have enough difficulty giving ourselves that permission without having to seek it from others.

All our lives we struggle with the need and desire for others' approval. From our first moments in life we learn how to win friends. We learn to smile, and say, "Yes," and

"Please," and "Thank you"—even when we don't feel like it. We rush to please parents and teachers, and later the boss and our loved ones.

Dan gave his family that approval, and when he asked for it in return, he paid the price. When he needed them they weren't there. He couldn't divorce his family, but he could free himself from a selfish woman who had no compassion. He could free himself from his wife. This was a painful double loss for Dan. Two women gone—but he knew it was the only way to survive.

In time, Dan found his tears. He took many long walks with his mother, and enjoyed the blessing of remembrance. And in time, he met and married a compassionate woman who joined him in his remembrance. Together, hand in hand, they stroll along the ocean's edge in silence. Dan turns and kisses his new wife's upturned face.

"Mother would have liked this."

WHICH WAY OUT?

I recently found myself in the Metropolitan Museum of Art in New York City, looking for the way out. I had been in these galleries a hundred times before—but now they were under construction. All the familiar guideposts were obscured by plywood paneling. Signs pointed in a variety of directions, with little or no indication of the exact destination I would reach if I followed them. I was reduced to following my instinct and hoping for the best.

As I took one unfamiliar turn after another, I became more and more anxious to find the exit. I seemed to be endlessly running in place, making no headway. Suddenly, I turned a corner and there was a familiar sight, the main stairway. From there I could find my way out. Find my way back home.

Looking back at that experience, I see how much like grief it was. Grief disorients us. That which was once familiar and easy to access seems blocked, and we feel trapped inside a labyrinth of wrong turns.

Grief often renders everything and everyone around us unfamiliar. Looking around our home we ask, "What place is this?" Friends and family become strangers we do not recognize and want nothing to do with. The guide-posts we can see promise nothing—they don't lead to any destination we want, and they won't release us from the confusion in the labyrinth that is grief.

• • •

Susan sits across from me with a steaming cup of tea poised at her lips. Her faraway look tells me that she has, for the moment, left me to relive a distant time. Tony has been dead three years, two months and ten days. Susan could tell you the hours, minutes, and seconds as well.

His death, while not sudden, was certainly unexpected. One day he was a robust forty-year-old man, and the next he was diagnosed with prostate cancer. He wasn't terminal, but he was in jeopardy. Susan and Tony were realistic. They faced the possibilities—and then they turned left and went into *denial*.

As the months passed, Tony recovered and seemed on the mend. He and Susan continued to eat well, exercise, and live the good life. One year later, new cancers were found throughout his body. His prognosis was terminal. They faced the possibilities—and then they turned left and went into *bargaining*, which took them straight into denial once more.

Welcome to the labyrinth.

Susan blinks, sips her tea, and finally looks up.

"I realize now that I was making deals—with God, with everybody, including Tony and myself. When the deal didn't work, I just ignored it and moved on to another deal—another doctor, another drug, another prayer. Finally, there was no choice but to accept the fact that Tony was dying, and there was no deal that could prevent that. We just sat together crying and holding on to each other for dear life. There's a telling phrase: *for dear life.*"

She brushed back a long curl from her forehead and heaved a deep sigh.

"What happened then?" I asked.

"He died." She sipped her tea again and carefully put the cup and saucer down on the coffee table. "I died."

"Or wanted to?" I quizzed.

"No, I never considered suicide. Not for an instant—even though I wanted to be dead. Wanted to be with Tony. I just wanted not to be living. It was too painful without him. I couldn't even get angry. All my rage was used up during his illness."

"So where are you now?"

"Still wandering around inside my grief. A pilgrim in search of answers, as you call it. Stuck, I guess." She looked down at the empty cup and then over at me. "Got any suggestions?"

I poured more tea.

• • •

Some people in the labyrinth don't really want to find the exit. Being lost—not being responsible—is a comfort in itself. To find the exit would mean coming home again, and with that the responsibility of reentering life, a life without your loved one. Holding on to dear life.

In the months that followed we drank a lot of tea, took a lot of wrong turns, and finally found the way out. Road-weary, bleary-eyed, and trembling, Susan blinked at the sunshine and stepped through the portal back into life.

Sometimes we can only find the way out by exploring all the alternate routes. Some of us need to examine and discard every possibility until we are finally convinced that this is, in fact, the real exit. Often, that journey is long and painful, but if we complete it—if we successfully traverse the labyrinth of grief—we can emerge on the far side and reenter life. We may never feel whole again, but we will feel healed.

• • •

I asked Susan how she had finally found the exit. She smiled.

"You know that I loved—still love—Tony, and I don't

think I will ever marry again. I don't even want to date. We were so much in love, so special together that it doesn't seem possible to me that I could ever love another man. I'm saying all this as a preface because I want you to understand what I'm going to tell you next." She brushed back her hair and smiled.

"Anyway, one afternoon last summer, I was coming back from the market and a man smiled at me. He couldn't have been a day over twenty-five. He simply smiled and said, 'Hello, pretty lady.' I almost laughed out loud, but instead I smiled back and hurried home. I felt strangely alive again. Then I realized that Tony used to call me that when we were dating. 'Pretty lady.' Isn't that silly? But it pulled me back into life in a way nothing else had. I wonder why?"

Maybe it was for the same reason that a chick knows the exact moment to start pecking at its eggshell. Life is an instinct.

THE SPOKEN WORD

I don't feel that there is any right or wrong way to do things—just right or wrong for each person. Sometimes I wish there were a set of guidelines or road maps to get us through the night, but I don't think there are.

But some things are so universal that they seem to work almost every time. This bit of advice I call "feel-good advice." It won't cure anything—it won't make the pain stop, or the sorrow go away forever—but it will definitely ease your pain and make you feel better.

Everyone I have ever talked with about grief and the way they deal with it says one thing again and again—they talk to the person who has died. In their minds there is a conversation that they feel will continue for the rest of their lives. I agree. I am in constant touch with all my loved ones who are gone. That's part of the honoring and remembering process. I let them know what's going on in my life, get their opinions, and toss around a few reactions and ideas. I tell them how I feel and how much I miss them. All this goes on inside my brain.

Now here is my advice. Speak these conversations out loud. No, not on the street, but in private.

I like to do it when I'm walking alone in the woods. The wind in the trees seems to be answering me. Or on the beach at dawn or dusk, when the swimmers and sunbathers have gone home, I walk along talking to my loved one and listening to the surf crash on the shore in response.

LIVING STATUES

Children seem to do this naturally—until they get caught by a parent and are discouraged from continuing. But it isn't crazy to do this, and it feels terrific. When you speak only in your mind there is no tone to the words. Sound gives it the richness of tone. You can hear your pain or your love or your joy or your sorrow. The spoken word has form and body and color.

Take my advice and go for a walk somewhere quiet. Talk out loud to your loved one who has died. Listen to the sound of your love and your sorrow and your joy in remembering. Then listen to the wind's response. Who knows? You might even get a message back.

LIVING STATUES

My childhood during the late 1930s and early 1940s was filled with magic and wonder. Long summer afternoons were often filled with a game of "Living Statues."

The rules were simple, as the best rules are. You held another player by the wrists and swung him around in circles, until you thought you had achieved the right balance of momentum and dizziness. Then you let go and sent your partner whirling off in free fall. At the precisely right moment, you shouted "*Freeze!*" The person you swung had to stop instantly and become a living statue.

Our front yard was always filled with frozen statues of young boys and girls trying not to lose their balance, or giggle. There wasn't any real point to this game, no winners or losers—just players having a moment of whimsy and delight.

There is a group of children on Long Island who belong to a workshop for grieving called Kids Have Feelings, Too. They get together to share their experiences as survivors of sibling death. Like widows, they have lost a partner, their brother or their sister.

Once, as we sat together and talked, I was struck by the silence that held so many of them in its grip. Their grief had struck them dumb. We sat in a circle, as we do in Harmony, and took turns talking—but this group seemed more silent than any I had ever met with before. Was it, I wondered, the nature of the group or the nature of their grief?

I watched their body language. Those who were silent were also very still—too still for children. They were far away, unreachable by sight or sound, held fast by the torment of unyielding sorrow. Like the children on the front yard of my home all those years ago, they had become living statues.

After more than two hours of talking, half the group remained stone-silent. The time had come to close for the evening. I asked them to hold hands and do an exercise of remembrance. "This," I explained to them, "lets us honor the one we love by saying one word that brings back a memory of that person."

"Must I explain the word?" asked one girl.

"No," I replied, "the memory word is like a secret code word that only you know the real, true meaning of."

They had never done anything like this before, and I could feel the tension building as they searched their minds for a key word that would trigger their memory. Something, not too painful, that would jog loose a cherished moment. I started them off with a magical word of my own.

"Kapusta." It was the name of the yellow-eyed, slate-grey cat who came to live with me after Greg died. I smiled when I said the word—I knew they wouldn't understand it and I let it linger as an example to them of just how mystical and obscure their memory word could be. Slowly, shyly, they began one after another to intone the magic word that would trigger their memories and grant them, for that moment, the gift of remembrance.

"Hamburgers."

"Whistle."

"Rock 'n' roll."

"Butterflies."

"Baseball."

"Rocks."

"Hugs."

"Snowflakes."

"Ocean."

"Bees."

When everyone had offered their word, we sat quietly for a moment or two. Then we went downstairs for milk and cookies. I could hear laughter as they tumbled down the stairs.

What I find interesting about this list of magic words is that it is almost identical to the ones spoken by widows. Perhaps grownups express it in more specific terms— "Ocean" might become "Fire Island"—but essentially they express the same thing, a remembrance that gives both pleasure and comfort, the comfort of release.

It is always just one word that says it all. And that word always means exactly the same thing: "I love you and I miss you." That's simply what grief is—missing the one you love.

And saying that out loud can bring a statue to life.

THE WORRY BONE

Over the years, I have had several cats, but only one dog—Nina.

Nina (for *Ninotchka*, the great Garbo film) was a blue-eyed Siberian husky that my friend Bruce talked me into buying. I had always loved wolves, and a husky seemed to be the domestic dog that looked most like a wolf. She was a difficult puppy, frisky to a frenzy, and as mischievous as a pixie.

There was a game we'd play that would delight her and wear me to a frazzle. She had a big red rubber bone with a bell inside it. Nina would bring her bone over to me and drop it at my feet—a mute invitation to pick it up and throw it for her to retrieve. A normal dog-and-foolish-human game.

But the moment I had my hand on the bone, Nina would swoop down and seize the other end in her jaws. The game was on. She'd growl and shake her head in a desperate attempt to get the bone away from me. The little bell inside tinkled frantically as we tugged against each other in this struggle for possession. And when I'd let go, she'd tumble backward, head over heels, still holding the bone between her teeth. For a few seconds she'd glare at me—then she'd trot back and drop the bone at my feet once again. She knew a fool when she saw one.

If I wouldn't play her game she'd pick up the bone herself, go off somewhere and chew on it, "worry" it, for hours. Because of Nina, when people say they are worried about something I tell them to stop chewing on their red rubber bone and get back into the game.

That's what Nina taught me about life. It's fun to worry a bone by yourself—especially if there's a little bell inside that can annoy everyone within earshot. But it's a lot more fun to worry a bone together and make it a game.

When someone you love dies, it means the end of the way things were. And we worry about all that. We worry about our grieving and our healing, and about letting go and moving on. We worry that we will forget to re-member. We worry that we will never again feel the joy of love, or of being loved. We linger and ponder and wonder and worry.

When I see that happening to someone, I tell the story about Nina and her red rubber bone. I tell about how after we had worried it together for awhile, I'd let go and she'd go tumbling over and I'd have the last laugh.

Somehow, magically, letting go gives us the last laugh

over worry. I don't know how it works, but I know that it does.

Thanks, Nina.

LINK BY LINK

One of the most devastating emotions after the death of a loved one is the feeling of isolation. No matter where you turn, or who you turn to, you still feel alone.

When new widows come into my groups they almost always talk about this aloneness, this sense of being cut loose and set adrift. The great loss of connection is very often coupled with a sense of being abandoned by the one most loved and trusted.

All too often this sense is expressed in phrases like, "When Sam left me," or, "After Bob went away." But our reluctance to say the word *death* often does more to enhance our aloneness than to diminish it. Difficult as it is to say, death at least gives us a sense of finality and completion. Those other expressions imply that we are somehow involved or responsible for Sam and Bob's departure. Once again it is important to face the truth and use the right words to describe what happened. Sam did not leave and Bob did not go away. They died.

After we hammer out this little exercise in linguistics, I usually ask the widows what they want to do next with their lives. Those who aren't frozen solid in their grief can join our forward movement exercise—the Widow's Chain.

When someone who has moved forward out of her grief and is ready to get back into life asks me what to do next, I often suggest that she place an ad in her local newspaper, or pin up a notice at the church or library that reads:

Widow Seeks Other Widows for Tea and Commonality

Very quickly she'll have a group. And one of the first things they'll all discover in that group is where each of them is in their journey back to life. Then they can form a chain and start bringing each other forward. Motion is the only way out of grief. When people feel that they want to get back into life, this is a good way to get going.

There is a wonderful organization called The Compassionate Friends, a nationwide network of groups of grieving parents. This network is the perfect example of a chain of healing. The members share, comfort, and challenge one another in their mutual grief. Their process, like the widows', is to forge a strong chain of healing—link by link.

Grief is a common ground where prince and pauper are equal in the face of death and loss. It is here, on this common ground, that we find our hearts—and sometimes our souls.

I recently heard a story about the AIDS quilt that is the perfect example of this commonality of grief. The quilt is composed of thousands of panels, each one honoring a loved one who has died of AIDS. The last time it was displayed, it covered an area of land equivalent to seven football playing fields. This sprawling, colorful commemoration is a tribute to the power of love.

There, among the brilliantly colored fabric panels, a young man came to mourn his lover's death—a death ignored by his own family and even his dead lover's family. Alone, and facing the same disease that had taken the one person who he felt had really loved him, he knelt and prayed to what he feared was an indifferent God. Silently, with tears streaming down his face, he asked God to protect and cherish his lover, to love him and forgive any sins he may have committed, and to grant him peace. Would God be listening?

As he waited for God to answer, he felt a hand touch

his shoulder and he turned to face the fragile figure of a grey-haired woman in her late 60s.

"This is my son next to your lover," she said. "Perhaps they are together watching us now. Let's wave to them." She took the young man's hand and lifted it skyward. Together they waved to their loved ones in heaven—their clasped hands forming a new link.

BUTTER

Usually, Harmony is a quiet, even serene, place. A meeting place where we can find the kind of compassion and understanding that seem to be missing in the outside world.

But like everything else in life, Harmony occasionally needs fine-tuning, sometimes even a major adjustment. One Wednesday-night gathering turned out to be a night for adjustment. My grandmother was fond of saying that, "life is a mirror that shows you your hat isn't on straight." Well, on that Wednesday night I was shown just how cock-eyed my cap was.

• • •

Rachel had been a widow for less than a year. After a few months of devastating mourning—she seldom got out of bed before noon and almost never left the house—Rachel's doctor sent her to see me.

Reluctantly, she visited our Wednesday night group of widows. Silently, she listened and observed without joining in. When we spoke our closing words of remembrance, she remained outside the circle. She left abruptly, with a simple thank-you to the group, and I thought that was the last we'd ever see her.

The following week Rachel appeared again as if nothing had happened. Once again she observed the group in silence, and once again she remained detached and aloof. At the end she thanked us and left. My curiosity was piqued, and I wondered what the odds were of her return. Most others in the group thought that she'd be back the next week. And she was.

In time, she became part of the group. But when the chain was formed at the closing she was always at the end—by her choice. Even after three months, she kept assigning herself the last link. Others who had joined the group after her were moving along. But Rachel insisted that she was still at the end of the chain.

One Wednesday evening, we had just finished breathing our way to Harmony.

The subject that night was honoring and remembering—how, after our loved one has died, we can remember and honor them with our life and our living. Susan had just begun to talk about some of her memories of her husband when Rachel suddenly stood up and started shouting.

"Stop it! Stop it!" she screamed at us. "Stop talking about remembering. I hate that!" She pulled at her sweater and wrung her hands, looking into our faces for someone who could confirm her emotions.

"What's the matter with you all? How can you talk about remembering? Where's your pain?" She stopped suddenly and faced me directly, her fingers spread wide in frustration and accusation. "Don't you get it? I don't want memories—I want my husband!"

It was a truth we all knew and lived with, but seldom spoke of. It was the very core of our grief.

A memory is a poor substitute for the real thing. A memory can't hold you in its arms or fill you with pleasure, or laugh at your jokes or pitch you a ball, or brag about your cooking and fight back unfairly, or surprise you on your birthday. In a world where the living are diamonds, memory is a paste imitation—a lackluster copy of the gleaming original.

No one wants a memory. We all want the real thing.

Rachel raged on for a few minutes more, and then, faced with our stunned silence, she sat down, hands folded primly in her lap, and waited for us to respond. I wondered who would answer her, and hoped it wouldn't have to be me because I didn't believe I had the words. Thankfully, Barbara did.

"For weeks now, Rachel, you've assigned yourself the last link in the chain and we let you. We let you because all of us have been there and don't really want to admit that we are moving along—making progress. Moving along seems like forgetting. Moving along seems like infidelity. Moving along says 'I have stopped caring and loving.' So we let you stay there for your own good and your own comfort.

"But tonight, dear friend, you have moved forward and you have brought us with you. You have said the words we all fear and hate and opened all the old wounds we thought were healing. Your rage gives meaning to your love and to ours."

She reached out her hand to Rachel. "Not one of us wants to settle for less than the real thing, but the real thing is gone. Margarine isn't the real thing. Butter is. But if there is no butter, then you make do with the next best thing.

"I don't want my life to be dry toast. I want it covered with rich golden butter. But my butter is gone, and all I have left is the memory of its richness, its pure golden quality, its sweet taste. The margarine of memory will never, ever, replace or even approximate the real thing. But, Rachel, it is far better than dry toast!

"Stewart is dead, Rachel, dead and buried and gone. Forever. Your butter is gone, just like mine is, and everyone else's in this room. All you have to do—all you *can* do now—is decide if you want the rest of your life to be dry toast."

In silence we all examined the loss of rich, golden butter in our lives and knew that it was the prospect of a life of dry toast that had brought us here together. There in Harmony we shared our recipes for a life, using margarine.

That night as we held hands and closed with our one word memory, I asked Rachel to start.

"Butter," she intoned.

"Butter."

"Butter."

"Butter."

"Butter."
"Butter."
"Butter."
"Butter."
"Butter."
"Butter."
"Butter." I completed the circle.

LIFE IS A BANQUET

One of my favorite movies is based on the Patrick Dennis novel, *Auntie Mame*. This joyous romp into the fantastic world of Mame Dennis and her young ward Patrick is every boy's dream of how to best discover the meaning of life and how to live it.

"Life is a banquet," intones Mame. "And most damn fools are starving to death." She implies that life is there for the taking, so don't hold back your plate.

In the film, Mame's beloved husband is killed in a mountain-climbing accident. We see Mame wearing a black high-necked dress of mourning. She is comforted by family and friends. Her grief is genuine.

But so is her lust for life. At the end of the scene she is called back to life by her friends. They remind her that the banquet awaits, and that too much grieving kills your appetite. She agrees with a laugh and turns her back to the camera. Suddenly, we see that the back of her mourning gown is cut in a deep V-shape, at the tip of which is a giant red cabbage rose. The lights fade until only a pinspot illuminates the rose on her fanny. The banquet is open once again.

Not all of us reenter life with the flair of Mame Dennis, but her example is valid. Her husband loved that capricious quality that could turn a mourning gown into a party dress. Wasn't she honoring him by continuing to live her life the way he had always wanted her to? Wasn't she saying she loved him by honoring that love? I think she was.

I'd certainly be pleased if someone I loved that much wore a flower on her fanny at my funeral.

THE WAILING WALL

One of the most difficult aspects of grief is confrontation. Sooner or later we must come to terms with a series of truths that are unbearable. The one we love is gone, and we are alone.

Slowly, we face these truths and deal with them. In time, we may find relief in tears and the healing effect they have.

Jerusalem has a wailing wall. In America, we have one, too—it is called the Vietnam War Memorial. No other conflict has filled this nation with more tears than the Vietnam war. To stand before this massive obsidian monument is to be filled with an overpowering sense of sorrow and loss. Truly, this is a wall to shed our tears upon.

Standing before that awesome black slab of stone, I think not only of my friends who died, but of those whose consciences would not let them fight in a war they believed immoral. They went to Canada and gave up their lives, and those who went to war and died lost theirs. Vietnam took many lives—the unaccounted-for soldiers in Vietnam are not the only MIAs. And so we lean against the stone cold wall and weep if we can.

Some ask why we erect these cold stone monuments instead of a glorious, flower-filled park. Why do we honor the dead with something so unfeeling as stone? Why not a living, blooming field of flowers and trees?

Perhaps we do it to induce tears. Standing again

before the marble facade inscribed with the names of warriors now gone, I look at the faces around me. Strained against the onslaught of their remembered sorrow they find release and comfort in tears.

A couple—she bent and white-haired, he, tall, erect, and stiff-necked like the ramrod officer he clearly once was, stands and gazes at the wall. Their eyes graze the surface and mentally touch each name until they find the one they seek.

They move forward, and he reaches out to touch the wall. I watch as he touches the name, fingers trembling, and suddenly, like a punctured balloon, all the wind goes out of him. A primal wail pierces the air as his knees buckle under him. She, trying to support him, is instead dragged down along with him.

Together, they fall sobbing against the wall. His hand is still on the spot where their son's name is engraved. This is the first time they could afford to make the journey here since the day the telegram arrived informing them of their only son's sacrifice. All the years of waiting to finally touch him again and say farewell have been without a father's tears. Now, crushed to the ground by overwhelming grief, he finds his tears. She, who has nearly dried up from crying, finds fresh ones to mingle with his.

I move beside them and wait until they seem ready to rise. Gently, I assist them. They have given up dignity for the sake of pride—the pride of love and loss. We walk up the knoll together, and later they share their son with me in stories and pictures.

"I was afraid I wouldn't live long enough to get here," he confesses. "I have a bad heart and the doctor said I shouldn't make the trip. But we've been planning it for so many years. I thank the Almighty for giving me the strength." She pats his hand and they exchange a lifetime in their glance. We hug and say goodbye.

Later, I return and find my friend's name. He is two rows and ten names down from their son. I introduce them by reaching out and touching both names. The stone wall is cold and chilling.

My tears are warm and comforting.

THE QUEST FOR WONDER

Lawrence Ferlinghetti, America's great bohemian poet, wrote a poem entitled "I Am Waiting" which appears in his 1955 collected work, *A Coney Island of the Mind.*

The poem, intended to be an oral message accompanied by jazz, chronicles the poet's desire for change in what seems to be an unchangeable world. He laments all that is wrong, and at the end of each stanza he declares, "I am perpetually awaiting a rebirth of wonder."

A rebirth of wonder.

When someone we love has died, we often seek a rebirth of wonder.

This quest is not an easy one. It means letting go of grief and reaching out for new life. It means forward movement, out of the paralyzing inertia of grief and into the activity of life. This is never easy, but it is essential—we must let go of the loved one who has died. We must accept that they are gone. We must deal with the pain of being left behind—feeling alone and abandoned.

Only after we let go of all that is negative, and refocus on what there is here and now, can we begin our new life. Only then will we receive the gift of remembrance and a rebirth of wonder.

EPILOGUE

At the beginning of this book we saw the image of people in a train station saying goodbye. You will recall that one woman squared her shoulders and headed straight back into life.

This is her story.

• • •

"My name is Helen. I am fifty-seven years old. I was a little girl, maybe seven, when my father was killed in the war. No one told me he was dead. They said he went away and someday he'd return. He never did.

"My cat died. My bird died. Several of my dolls died. And I buried them all under the peach tree in our back yard. I never cried.

"When I was seventeen I met Robert, who became my husband two years later. We had two children, Austin and Serena. When Austin was twelve, he drowned in a lake while he was at camp. It was over ten years before my rage subsided enough for me to find my tears for him.

"When Serena was sixteen she disappeared without a trace. We never saw or heard from her again. They never found her dead or alive. She simply vanished. I wonder about her every day. My husband never got over it. Two children gone—and my husband so withdrawn that he couldn't touch me or even look into my eyes.

"Our lives silently centered around our loss. In time, the loss became a wedge between us, driving us even further apart. We were of no comfort to each other, even though our loss was mutual.

"Four years ago, Robert was diagnosed with terminal cancer, and he was given six months to a year.

"At first we were too stunned to do much of anything. But as time passed we began to talk—maybe for the first time in our lives. Time was running out and we decided to make the most of it. Robert moved back into our bedroom, and every night he took me into his arms and held me until I fell asleep. When he was in his last months I held him the same way.

"We talked about our children and how much we had grieved for them. How much we still do. We cried together. We relived it all like an old newsreel and we found the good in it all. And we found God again. We had been so angry, felt so betrayed, that we had turned our backs on Him because we felt He had abandoned us.

"Somehow, through prayer, or positive thinking, or

just sheer stubbornness, Robert got himself three more years of life. They were the best three years of our life together. We enjoyed every single day to the fullest. Up at dawn and walking in the fresh morning air. Late to bed and cuddling under the covers like newlyweds. We even made love again like frightened sweethearts, we were very careful of one another, making sure the other was pleased.

"In the middle of his last year we saw it coming and each and every moment became precious. He wanted to die in my arms, and with the help of the local hospice we made that possible.

"Looking back on my life I see a fragile little girl who grew up into a nervous, shy girl, who married too young. I had no idea how difficult life could be, and when it knocked me down I didn't believe I had the strength to survive—but I did.

"In those last days of Robert's life we laughed so much I thought I'd wet my pants. The nurses didn't know what to make of us. For years our laughter had been overshadowed by our grief. We hurt too much to laugh. Now, as death approached, we found a million things to laugh about. Moment after moment of silliness that had gone unnoticed was brought back, relived, and laughed about. Robert died smiling.

"After he died, right after the funeral, actually, I packed my suitcase and went to the Grand Canyon. It was what we had decided I should do. Neither of us had ever been there, but we had both always dreamed about it. Robert said that if I went and looked at that great big beautiful hole in the earth it would make the hole in my life seem insignificant. Of course, he was just kidding. He knew that the Grand Canyon was just a rut in the road by comparison to the depth of my longing to be held one more time in his arms. But he was a modest man.

"Now that I'm back from the Grand Canyon, I realized that looking across that vast crater I could still see the other side. That was an important sight. For now, I know that I can see across the vast chasm of my grief as well. And I know in my heart that there *is* life on the other side. I can build a bridge across it, or I can walk around the perimeter of it, but sooner or later I'm going to get there.

"I watched the sun set one night at the canyon. Its golden hues colored the far side of the canyon—and then, in the morning, I watched the sun rise and color the opposite side. I was standing on that side as the sun came up. It bathed me in its golden light.

"I felt warm inside for the first time since Robert died."

RESOURCES

My lifelong friend and gentle mentor, Florence Mills, was the town's librarian when I was suffering from acne and puberty in Baldwin, Long Island. My hunger for knowledge coupled with a passion for books had led me to her. She responded by filling my arms with books and my head with endless possibilities.

I remember someone saying something like: "Intelligence isn't knowing *what* the answer is but knowing *where* the answer is." "Millsie," and the Dewey Decimal System provided me with the *where* of intelligence—a gateway to all that was wonderful.

There are millions and millions of ways to grieve, one for each death, for each individual experiencing loss, for each long goodbye. There are three sources of information right in your own home and neighborhood as you search for the *where* of grief. The first is your own phone book, which will list hotlines and groups that offer helping hands. Another resource will be your local newspaper, or "pennysaver," which will also list groups of interest. And, of course, your public library, which not only has thousands of books but a wealth of catalogs and guides that list organizations and professionals that can assist you.

I'd like to paraphrase that little saying about intelligence: "Wisdom is not knowing what the answer is, but knowing where the answer is—it is in your own heart."

Everything else is a guide. There are many guidebooks and organizations to help you with your journey. Here are a few of them.

BOOKS

Branden, Nathaniel. *Honoring the Self*. New York: Bantam Books, 1985.

———. *The Disowned Self*. New York: Bantam Books, 1973.

> These books are not specifically directed towards grieving, but they offer helpful advice for overcoming loss.

Caine, Lynne. *Widow*. New York: Bantam Books, 1987.

> In this classic, Lynne Caine explains how to overcome the anger and pain of widowhood. Though out of print, copies may be found at your library.

Callanan, Maggie and Kelley, Patricia. *Final Gifts: Understanding the Special Awareness, Needs, and Communications of the Dying*. New York: Poseidon Press, 1992.

> Written by hospice nurses, this book deals with the dying and their final messages of love—and how we can receive and understand them.

Colgrove, Melba, Ph.D., Harold H. Bloomfield, M.D., and Peter McWilliams. *How to Survive the Loss of a Love*. Los Angeles: Bantam/Prelude Press, 1991.

> This poetic, comforting guidebook describes the stages of loss, and provides ways of recovering from losses of all kinds. This edition is a revision of the first edition, published in 1976.

Ilse, Sheroke, and Elizabeth Levang, Ph.D. *Remembering With Love: Messages of Hope for the First Year of Grieving and Beyond*. Minneapolis, MN: Deaconess Press, 1992.

> A gentle question and answer format guides the reader along the pathway of grieving.

Kübler-Ross, Elisabeth. *AIDS: The Ultimate Challenge*. New York: Collier Books, 1987.

———. *On Children and Death*. New York: Collier Books, 1985.

———. *On Death and Dying*. New York: Collier Books, 1970.

———. *Questions and Answers on Death and Dying*. New York: Collier Books, 1985.

> *On Death and Dying* is still the definitive study of grieving and the process of death. Dr. Kubler-Ross's other books focus on death in specific situations involving children and persons with AIDS.

Kushner, Harold S. *When Bad Things Happen to Good People*. New York: Avon Books, 1983.

> Recounting the story of a family's struggle with a son's terminal illness, this book provides powerful, compassionate, and comforting answers to the question, "Why me?"

Lukas, Christopher, and Henry M. Seiden, Ph.D. *Silent Grief: Living in the Wake of Suicide*. New York: Bantam Books, 1990.

> This book, written for survivors of suicide, includes a resources section organized by state.

MacLaine, Shirley. *Dancing in the Light*. New York: Bantam Books, 1986.

> In her personal saga, Ms. MacLaine explores reincarnation and the idea of continuation.

Matthews-Simonton, Stephanie, and Robert L. Shook. *The Healing Family*. New York: Bantam Books, 1989.

> A positive approach to how families can work together to create a healing environment when a family member is facing a life-threatening disease.

Morse, Melvin, Ph.D., with Paul Perry. *Closer to the Light*. New York: Villard Books, 1990.

> The authors examine the near-death experiences of children and adults, focusing on the vision of a clean, loving, white space that awaits us.

BOOKS FOR CHILDREN

Buscaglia, Leo. *The Fall of Freddie the Leaf*. New York: Henry Holt, 1982.

Greenlee, Sharon. *When Someone Dies*. Atlanta, GA: Peachtree Publishers, Ltd., 1992.

POETRY

Greene, Vivian. *Good Mourning*. New York: Mirrors, 1992.

> A collection of inspirational poems about life and death and the experience of grief.

HOTLINES

Check your telephone book for local numbers and organizations.

HOSPICELINK (hospice care) 1–800–331–1620

KIDWATCH HOTLINE (missing children) 1–800–451–9422

NATIONAL AIDS HOTLINE 1-800-342-2437

YOUTH CRISIS AND RUNAWAY HOTLINE 1–800–448–4663

SERVICE ORGANIZATIONS

There are many national groups for those who are grieving, with local chapters. One of the largest is THE COMPASSIONATE FRIENDS, a support group for parents whose children have died. Almost every community has smaller groups that have been formed to help one another, and they are usually listed in local directories and newspapers.

THE NAMES PROJECT FOUNDATION
2362 Market Street, San Francisco, CA 94114
(415) 863–5511

> The Names Project sponsors the international AIDS memorial quilt and raises funds for people with AIDS and their loved ones. Chapters across the country and affilitates around the world offer assistance and materials for making a memorial quilt panel.

> If you would like to ask a question or share an experience,
> please feel welcome to write to me, c/o:
> The Harmony Project
> Box 28K
> 300 East 40th Street
> New York, NY 10016